21ST
CENTURY
DEBATES

AIR POLLUTION
OUR IMPACT ON THE PLANET

MATTHEW CHAPMAN
AND ROB BOWDEN

RAINTREE
STECK-VAUGHN
RSVP® PUBLISHERS

A Harcourt Company

Austin New York
www.raintreesteckvaughn.com

21st Century Debates Series

Genetics • Surveillance • Internet • Media • Climate Change • Energy • Rain Forests
Waste, Recycling, and Reuse • Endangered Species • Food Supply • An Overcrowded World?

Published by Raintree Steck-Vaughn Publishers, an imprint of the Steck-Vaughn Company

**Library of Congress Cataloging-in-Publication Data
is available upon request.**

ISBN 0-7398-4874-7

Printed in Italy. Bound in the United States.

1 2 3 4 5 6 7 8 9 0 LB 06 05 04 03 02

Picture acknowledgments: Associated Press AP 56; Corbis 33; Ecoscene 6 (Ian Booth), 13 (Peter Currell), 37 (Eva Miessler), 39, 51 (Chinch Gryniewicz), 41 (Erik Schaffer), 48, 59 (Bruce Harber), 52 (Sally Morgan), 53 (Anthony Cooper); Eye Ubiquitous 11 (R. Friend), 30 (L. Fordyce); Angela Hampton Family Life Picture Library 27; Robert Harding 9 (Ken Sherman), 34 (Occidor Ltd); Impact Photos 32 (John Arthur), 44 (Mark Henley); Popperfoto 24, 25 & cover foreground (Jason Reed); Popperfoto/Reuters 20, 26, 46, 50, 57; Still Pictures 4 (Nigel Dickinson), 7 (John Isaac), 10, 29, 38 (Mark Edwards), 12 (Tony Crocetta), 15 (Andre Maslennikov), 16 (Mark Edwards), 17 (Roland Seitre), 18 (G. Griffiths–Christian Aid), 19 (Arnold Newman), 28 (Hartmut Schwarzbach), 31 (Reinhard Janke), 36 (Jorgen Schytte), 55 (Tantyo Bangun), 58 (Peter Arnold), cover background (Ray Pfortner); Wayland Picture Library 23, 49. The carbon cycle (4) and the radioactive fallout from Chernobyl (43) are both adapted from diagrams in *An Introduction to Sustainable Development* by J. Elliott, Routledge, 1999. The catalytic converter (45) is adapted from a diagram in *Philips Concise Encyclopedia*, 1998.

Cover: foreground picture shows an Indonesian family protecting themselves from air pollution; background picture shows a paper mill in New York State.

CONTENTS

THE AIR POLLUTION DEBATE

Upsetting the Balance

The air we breathe is essential for our survival; in fact, air is essential for almost all life on earth. But human actions over the last two centuries now pose a serious threat to our planet's life-giving atmosphere. Rapid population growth and industrialization have changed the balance between people and the natural environment. As we begin the 21st century, there is a real danger that the natural systems we often take for granted will begin to fail. One such system is the atmosphere, which controls our climate and the air we breathe. According to many scientists, the atmosphere is now so polluted that we may have to face catastrophic events over the next 100 years. These events could change the way we live forever.

What is Air Pollution?

Air pollution is the emission of chemicals or materials into the atmosphere. Smoke from a fire, dust from a building site, and gas fumes from a stove are all forms of air pollution. Even smells and noises are types of air pollution. But not all air pollution comes from human activities. Forest fires, dust storms, decaying vegetation, volcanic eruptions, and even termites have produced large quantities of air pollution for thousands of years. In the past, these pollutants have been controlled by natural cycles (e.g., the carbon cycle, opposite).

Traffic congestion is a major human source of air pollution. This is the rush hour in Manila, capital of the Philippines.

But human activities have increased the levels of air pollution so dramatically that these cycles may no longer be able to cope. Most of the air pollution produced by humans comes from power plants, factories, motor vehicles, and the clearing of land for farming.

Air Pollutants

The chemicals or materials that cause air pollution are known as pollutants. Some of these are obvious, like the black diesel smoke from a bus or truck, or the white trails left by jet aircraft in the sky. However, many pollutants cannot be seen or smelled even though they may be just as damaging. Special equipment is needed to detect these pollutants so that we know when air pollution levels become dangerous. These periods are called air pollution episodes. Using modern technology, scientists are able to warn us about pollution episodes in the same way as a weather forecaster warns of heavy rain.

VIEWPOINTS

"As air quality is both a local and global issue... regional and international efforts to control air pollution are of increasing importance."
Dr. Devra L. Davis, World Resources Institute, and Dr. Paulo Saldiva, University of Sao Paulo

"The Earth's climate has never been fixed and human impact on climate has been relatively minor compared to naturally occurring large-scale perturbations."
Nick Middleton, Geographical Magazine, United Kingdom

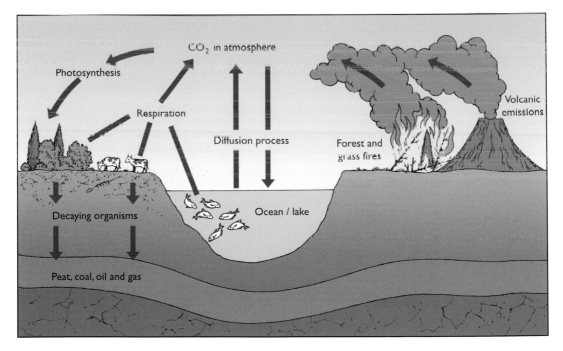

Natural systems, such as the carbon cycle, are being put under increasing pressure by human emissions.

FACT

A child born in New York, Paris, or London will consume, pollute, and waste more in their lifetime than fifty children born in a developing country.

Tourism could be affected as historic buildings, such as the Acropolis in Athens, are eroded by acid rain and urban air pollution.

VIEWPOINTS

"Only a few million people in China now own private cars, but that number could rise to 400 million in fifty years, as the country's population tops 1.5 billion."
Scott Elliott, Los Alamos National Laboratory, New Mexico

"Population growth is at the heart of the pollution problem as nations attempt to provide the energy, food, products, fresh water, sanitation, housing, and transportation needed and desired by the growing urban populations."
Derek Elsom, Professor of Climatology, Oxford Brookes University, United Kingdom

Origins of Air Pollution

Human air pollution can be traced back to ancient Rome and Greece. This was when people first began to live in cities, and the high number of wood fires in a relatively small space caused poor air quality locally. However, it was the greater use of coal in the Industrial Revolution in 19th-century Europe and North America that started the large-scale air pollution problems we face today.

Since the 20th century, controls have been introduced to reduce air pollution. As a result, the air in industrial cities like Detroit, Michigan or Manchester, England, is much cleaner at the beginning of the 21st century than it was at the start of the 20th. However, world population increased from 1.65 billion to 6 billion over the same century, placing great pressure on natural resources such as the atmosphere.

This pressure is likely to grow, because developing countries—despite their high populations—currently account for a very small proportion of global air pollution. If these countries develop standards of living similar to North America or Europe, environmentalists warn that we will need about eight planets to support us all!

What Can Be Done?

Despite all these problems, we can reduce air pollution. Scientists are continually developing new forms of energy (such as solar, wave, and hydrogen power) to lessen our dependence on polluting fossil fuels like coal and oil. Technological developments have made products more efficient, and improved building techniques have made buildings less polluting.

There is a lot that we can each do personally, such as walking or cycling instead of traveling in a car, or recycling bottles and cans to save the energy used in the manufacturing of raw materials. Even turning off unnecessary lights could make a big difference. A good starting point is to understand more about air pollution. This book will help you do that, so that you can make your own decisions about the best way to tackle the problem.

VIEWPOINT

"Children said that if they were in charge, they would do more to help the environment than adults currently do. One quarter of the children felt that the grown-ups were not taking care of the environment very well and could do much better."
Department of the Environment. Transportation and Regions (DETR) United Kingdom website

In 1990, withdrawing Iraqi troops set fire to Kuwaiti oil fields, turning the skies black with pollution for weeks. Specialist teams from the United States and Europe were sent to put out the fires.

DEBATE

Before you continue, think about the different sources of air pollution in your own everyday life. Perhaps you could list some of these sources along with actions to take to reduce them.

THE POLLUTANTS

A Chemical Soup

The earth's atmosphere is made up of many different chemicals or "ingredients." These combine in differing amounts to make a giant "chemical soup." The main ingredients of the air we breathe are the gases nitrogen (78.09 percent), oxygen (20.9 percent), argon (0.93 percent), hydrogen (0.05 percent) and carbon dioxide (0.03 percent), with smaller quantities of other gases, particles, and water vapor.

These ingredients remain remarkably stable. But, just as adding spices to a bowl of soup will change its flavor, any ingredients introduced into the air can change the character of our atmosphere. This is why air pollution presents a problem.

Where Do Pollutants Come From?

At present, there are lots of different types of air pollutants with new ones still being discovered and created. These can come from natural or human sources and sometimes from both. For example, methane is produced by rotting waste in man-made landfill sites, but it is also produced naturally by decomposing organic matter (such as vegetation or animal waste). This makes it difficult to tell which source is more responsible.

Many pollutants can be traced to a specific pollution source, such as car exhaust fumes or a fire. These are known as "primary pollutants" and we can think of their source as either natural or human. Several major pollutants, however, such as ozone, are "secondary pollutants" produced by chemical reactions in the atmosphere. Their source can be harder to trace, but because they mostly originate from primary sources, we can focus on these as a priority.

Natural sources include forest fires, dust storms, swamps, and decomposing organic waste. Volcanoes are a particularly important natural source—a single eruption can release enough pollutants to change the earth's atmosphere and weather patterns for several years. We cannot control these natural sources; they have always produced pollutants. Some scientists even believe that natural pollutants caused the extinction of the dinosaurs some 55 million years ago.

Human sources include exhaust fumes from vehicles, smoke from factories, and the waste gases produced by heating our homes, schools, and offices. These man-made sources increased dramatically during the 20th century, due to rapid population growth and the development of new materials and products. Many of these products led to the creation of new pollutants, such as chlorofluorocarbons (CFCs) used in refrigerators and aerosol sprays. However, unlike natural sources, we can control human pollution sources by changing the way we live and behave.

FACT

When Mount Pinatubo erupted in the Philippines in June 1991, it threw ash 19.2 miles (32 kilometers) into the atmosphere and caused a temporary lowering of global temperatures for more than two years.

Our dependence on fossil fuels, being processed in the form of oil in Kentucky, is blamed for many of today's environmental problems, especially global warming.

FACT

CO₂ emissions have increased by nearly 30 percent since the beginning of the Industrial Revolution, methane concentrations have almost tripled, and nitrous oxide concentrations have risen by 15 percent.

Monitoring Air Pollution

Some air pollutants are easy to identify, such as smoke which is visible or ammonia which has a very strong smell. But many, including some of the most hazardous, are invisible and have no smell. Scientists have developed special equipment to detect and monitor these pollutants. This can vary from simple detectors placed in our homes to warn of poisonous carbon monoxide to multi-million dollar satellites that observe changes in the earth's ozone layer from space. Monitoring also helps us understand where pollution comes from and how it is affected by our behavior and lifestyles.

Installing monitoring equipment in European cities such as Copenhagen has improved our understanding of air pollution and has made these cities healthier places to live.

To monitor all air pollutants, however, would be difficult and expensive. For this reason, scientists have traditionally focused their attention on six main pollutants known to cause particular harm to people and environments. These six are sulphur dioxide, nitrogen oxides, ozone, carbon monoxide, particulate matter, and lead.

Clean air laws have dramatically reduced certain pollutants. This gas station in Las Vegas, Nevada, checks exhaust emissions and services polluting vehicles.

Traditional Air Pollutants

Sulphur dioxide (SO_2) is produced when we use fossil fuels, such as coal and oil. But it also occurs naturally as organic matter decomposes and when volcanoes erupt. In 1860, SO_2 emissions were around 10 million tons per year but by the mid-1980s this had risen dramatically to 150 million tons per year. Countries such as Canada, the United States, the United Kingdom, and Germany were among the biggest polluters, due to their rapid industrial growth. However, since the 1980s, many developed nations have halved their SO_2 emissions. Now it is developing countries, such as China and India, which are becoming the bigger polluters.

Nitrogen oxides (NOx) are also produced by the burning of fossil fuels. Although NOx are found in nature, human activities are the main source. Internal combustion engines used in motor vehicles account for around 50 percent of emissions, while industry contributes a further 25 percent. Some forms of NOx can be toxic to humans, making breathing difficult and having a particularly bad effect on asthma sufferers.

Natural pollution sources such as this sandstorm in Mali, West Africa, turn the air so thick with particulates that you can barely see or breathe.

Particulate matter, such as dust, soot, smoke, and other particles released into the atmosphere, is often overlooked as a pollutant. Yet it is one of the worst pollutants being generated today by factories, motor vehicles, fires, and even natural winds (as more land is cleared of vegetation, the soil can easily be picked up as dust).

These particles can be extremely small and are measured in micrometers (μm) which are a thousand times smaller than a millimeter (0.04 inches)! Particles as small as 2.5μm are regularly monitored and are known to cause severe breathing difficulties, especially for asthmatics and the elderly or young. Cities in the developing world are particularly polluted—Cairo, in Egypt, recorded levels up to ten times higher than those in the World Health Organization's recommended guidelines.

Newer Air Pollutants
New technologies have unfortunately created new pollutants such as hydrocarbons, Toxic Organic Micropollutants (TOMPs), and CFCs. These are usually produced in smaller quantities than traditional pollutants, but can be far more hazardous.

Hydrocarbons are a family of toxic air pollutants containing carbon and hydrogen used in fuels, paints, solvents, and cleaning products. They are often better known as volatile organic compounds (VOCs) and polycyclic aromatic hydrocarbons (PAHs). Hydrocarbons enter the air by evaporation or when products containing them are not properly incinerated. When combined with oxygen, they can irritate the skin and eyes, make you feel sick or dizzy, and are also known to cause cancer.

TOMPs are another family of pollutants, one of the most important being Polychlorinated Biphenyls (PCBs). Until recently, they were used in the manufacturing of electrical goods and industrial fluids. If not fully destroyed by incinerators operating at over 1200°C, products containing PCBs release toxins known to cause birth defects and cancer.

FACT

In 1976, the European Community banned the use of toxic PCBs in unsealed equipment. However, they are still faced with the problem of how to dispose of old or damaged equipment.

FACT

Even though global CFC production has fallen significantly, production actually rose by 87 percent in developing countries between 1986 and 1993.

Aerosols became a symbol of air pollution in the early 1990s. The ozone-depleting propellants they used to contain are now being phased out.

CFCs were developed in the 1930s for use in solvents, coolants (e.g., refrigerators) and propellants (e.g., aerosol sprays). When released into the atmosphere, CFCs destroy the ozone and contribute to global warming. Developed countries banned the use of CFCs in new products in 1999, but many developing countries are still using them until they can afford to develop alternatives.

DEBATE

Should we continue to develop new technologies (which may result in new pollutants) when we have not yet learned how to control some of the traditional pollutants we produce?

INTERNATIONAL AIR POLLUTION

A Global Problem

Although some air pollutants are limited to their immediate environment, others affect people and places hundreds of miles away. Many scientists now believe these pollutants are changing the climate of the whole planet. A smaller group of scientists suggest that climate change is a natural process, and they point to the large quantities of pollutants such as carbon dioxide and sulphur dioxide produced by natural sources. However, most scientists now agree there is a real danger that human actions and the air pollution they produce could severely alter our climate. The real debate is how serious these changes could be and who is responsible for them?

Trans-boundary Air Pollution

The air currents that produce our daily weather also carry pollutants over great distances. When pollution travels between countries like this it is known as trans-boundary air pollution because it crosses beyond the borders (or boundaries) of the country it originated in. Trans-boundary air pollution means that people and environments in far-off places are affected by pollutants that they have not produced themselves. For example, polar bears and the Inuit people who live in the Arctic have levels of chemical contamination that are among the highest in the world, even though they live thousands of miles from where the chemicals originate. Scientists have shown that this is because pollutants become concentrated in the blubber of the seals that both polar bears and Inuit people rely on for food.

Trans-boundary air pollution could be reduced if the countries involved cooperated with one another to monitor and control the pollutants. However, this can be very complicated to organize. Some countries may not be as willing as others to take responsibility, particularly if they are less affected by the problem.

FACT

Around 20 percent of forests and lakes in Scandinavia are dead and another 30 percent have been badly affected, mostly by air pollution (acid deposition) from other countries.

Acid Rain

Acid rain was one of the first types of trans-boundary air pollution to be widely noticed—in the 1970s. It is formed when sulphur dioxide and nitrogen dioxide mix with water vapor in the clouds. When this falls to the ground it damages plants and animals. It has been responsible for killing entire lake ecosystems in some countries, such as Canada and Norway. It also kills trees. For example, trees in Poland have lost over half their leaves due to acid damage. And in neighboring Germany it is predicted that 90 percent of trees will die over the next few decades due to the effects of acid rain.

These trees in Krkonose National Park, Poland, have been destroyed by acid rain. Eastern Europe has been particularly affected by this form of air pollution.

Liming helps neutralize the acid but is very expensive. It's better to reduce emissions.

FACT

One molecule of CFC can result in the loss of 100,000 ozone molecules.

FACT

Human emissions of CO_2 were around 3 million tons at the start of the Industrial Revolution in 1751. In 1998 we emitted around 6,400 million tons.

In Sweden, helicopters have been used to spread lime into acidified lakes to neutralize the acid and restore life in them. Over 5,500 lakes have been quite successfully treated in this way. But when acid rain falls on land and enters the underground water system, it is much harder to control.

In some areas of the United States, rainwater can be approximately 1000 times more acidic that natural rainwater, threatening erosion to our national monuments made of marble or limestone. Many famous buildings have been affected by acid rain. These include St. Paul's Cathedral in London, the Acropolis in Athens, and the Taj Mahal in India.

The problem with acid rain and other trans-boundary pollution is first, finding out who produces it, then, deciding who should pay for the damage it causes. For example, most of Japan's acid rain comes from air pollution originating in China. But does this mean that China should pay for damage in

Japan? In fact, Japan is helping China to pay for pollution control equipment to cut its emissions, in the hope that this will reduce acid rain damage in Japan. However, not all countries are so cooperative. In the 1980s, for instance, Britain took little responsibility for its emissions across Scandinavia despite complaints from the Norwegian government.

Global Warming

Perhaps the most serious type of trans-boundary air pollution is the release of greenhouse gases because this affects the whole earth. These gases include carbon dioxide, methane, and nitrous oxide. They occur naturally in the atmosphere and help to keep our planet warm by trapping energy from the sun. This is what we call the greenhouse effect.

However, since the Industrial Revolution, the burning of fossil fuels and other human activities have released more of these gases into the atmosphere and upset the natural balance. In the last fifty years chlorofluorocarbons (CFCs) have added to these gases, as well as damaging the ozone layer in the stratosphere, which protects the earth from harmful ultraviolet radiation.
With more energy reaching the earth, and more

VIEWPOINTS

"In 1990, 49 Nobel Prize winners and 700 members of the National Academy of Sciences said there is broad agreement among scientists that the growing greenhouse effect has the potential to produce dramatic changes in the climate."
Environmental Protection Agency (EPA)

"The most important greenhouse gases—carbon dioxide, methane, water vapor, and nitrous oxide—all occur naturally in the atmosphere, and without their greenhouse properties, the Earth's average temperature would be about 33°C lower than at present"
Nick Middleton, Geographical Magazine, United Kingdom

Meteorologists in Antarctica release special balloons to monitor the ozone hole. During the 1990s, the hole grew bigger every year.

FACT

Australia and the United Kingdom experienced their worst flooding for fifty years during November 2000. Some commentators believe this is a sign of global warming and warn us to expect more of such events around the world in future.

greenhouse gases to trap it in our atmosphere, our planet is getting warmer. Scientists believe the earth's surface could be 2 to 3°C warmer by the year 2100, causing major changes to our environment. We already appear to be seeing the results: 1997 and 1998 were the warmest years since records began. And in the polar regions, large sections of ice are beginning to melt away.

Current predictions suggest that this could cause sea levels to rise by 1.64 feet (0.5 meters) by 2100. If this happens coastal areas in countries such as England, the United States, the Netherlands, and Bangladesh could be seriously flooded, and some islands in the Pacific and Indian Oceans could disappear altogether. Even if we avoid large-scale flooding, scientists are warning that there will be many changes to our environment and the way we live.

Agriculture could be dramatically affected. Crops such as wheat and rice may grow better in the warmer temperatures, but others—like corn and sugar cane—won't. This may lead to changes in people's diets as different crops become more suited to being grown in different parts of the world. Rainfall may become less reliable, with sudden floods and prolonged droughts seriously affecting crop growth. Irrigation can solve this problem but it tends to be expensive and wasteful. Often, less than 20 percent of the water actually gets to the plants. On the other hand, the higher levels of carbon dioxide (which are partly responsible for global warming) are expected to increase the speed at which plants grow

Greater flooding associated with climate change could lead to more regular destruction of farmland such as here in the Tana River Valley, Kenya.

and so agriculture could improve. In reality, we don't know exactly what will happen, but we can expect to see crop production increase in some areas and decrease in others.

Wildlife may also be affected, with certain species having to migrate or face extinction due to changes in their environment. Naturalists have already noticed that some birds are migrating later due to warmer temperatures and in Costa Rica's MonteVerde Rain Forest the recent extinction of the Golden Toad is thought to be due to global warming. The ecosystems most at risk from these changes are tropical forests, coral reefs, deserts, polar regions, coastal marshes, mountains, and low-lying areas. Warmer temperatures will also affect our health by

The Golden Toad may be the first of many extinctions caused by atmospheric pollution and global warming.

increasing air pollution, as some cities will experience more sunshine and less rainfall, which will produce more photochemical air pollution episodes from pollutants such as ozone. This will make life very hard for people with respiratory illnesses such as asthma and bronchitis. Diseases such as malaria could increase, as

VIEWPOINT

"Climate change is generally considered a 'northern' issue. How do you convince people with more immediate problems that they should be concerned about the gradual warming of the earth?"
Annie Brisibe. Friends of the Earth. Nigeria. Central Africa

FACT

Studies have shown that SO_2 pollution can travel distances of up to 1,243 miles (2,000 kilometers) in just three to five days.

This NASA image shows the largest ozone hole seen to date as a large blue area over Antarctica and the southern tip of South America.

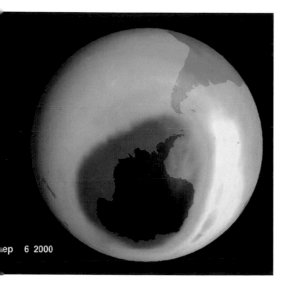

ep   6 2000

mosquitoes spread over a larger area in the new warmer climates. At present, just under half of the world's population lives in places where malaria exists, but scientists predict this could rise to 70 percent by 2070. On a more positive note, warmer temperatures might reduce the number of deaths from illnesses related to cold weather such as influenza. But the harm that global warming could cause would far outweigh this benefit.

A Global Response?

In response to warnings about global warming, 162 nations met at the 1992 Earth Summit in Rio de Janeiro, Brazil. In the Framework Convention on Climate Change, they agreed to implement national policies to reduce emissions, and share information about how to best reduce emissions without damaging economic development.

In 1997, at a second meeting in Kyoto, Japan, the same countries agreed to reduce greenhouse gas emissions to 5.2 percent below 1990 levels by the year 2012. Some countries are trying to do more than this; for instance, the United Kingdom aims to cut emissions by 20 percent by 2010. Such measures have been welcomed by environmentalists. But many of them say that even if bigger cuts were made immediately they would make little difference, due to the level of gases already in the atmosphere. CFCs, for example, can stay in the atmosphere for up to 100 years.

One problem is that not all countries are equally responsible for emissions. For example, on average, one American produces equivalent levels of CO_2 emissions to 7 Chinese, 24 Nigerians or 31 Pakistanis.

Main Greenhouse Gases from Human Activities

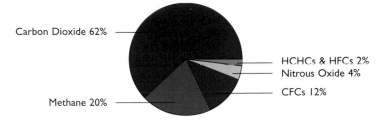

Carbon Dioxide 62%

HCHCs & HFCs 2%
Nitrous Oxide 4%
CFCs 12%

Methane 20%

Source: Atmospheric Research and Information Center

In addition, many of the poorer countries feel they need more time to reduce their emissions because of the extra cost involved in changing to newer, cleaner technologies. For this reason, European targets to reduce SO_2 emissions by 70 to 80 percent by the year 2000 (from 1980 levels) were lowered to 40 to 50 percent for the poorer countries of Eastern Europe.

Despite reductions in emissions, environmentalists argue that the only real solution is to start making greater use of alternative, sustainable energy sources, such as solar power and wind power.

DEBATE

Is it fair that countries producing high levels of air pollution should harm those that produce less, through effects such as acid rain or global warming? How would you persuade the more polluting countries to take greater responsibility for their actions?

World Carbon Dioxide Emissions 1980 and 1999

Million tons of carbon equivalent

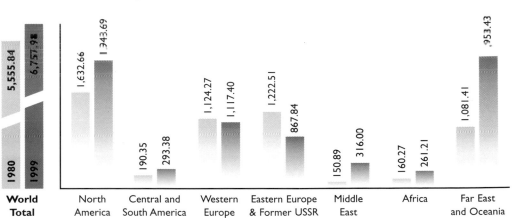

Source: U.S. Energy Information Administration (EIA)

NATIONAL AIR POLLUTION

A National Problem?

Air pollution at the national level can be easier to control than international and trans-boundary pollution, because individual countries can set and enforce their own pollution laws. In Denmark, for example, a green tax was introduced in July 1997 to encourage car owners to use more fuel-efficient cars and therefore cut down on air pollution. Those cars that use a lot of fuel are taxed more than those that can travel long distances on a little fuel.

However, not all countries are prepared to take responsibility for the pollution they produce, especially if they are not greatly affected by the pollutants themselves. Poorer nations may find it difficult to pay for cleaner technologies and are often more concerned with developing their economies than with the pollution their economic growth may generate.

Who Are the Polluters?

The air pollution produced by individual nations varies dramatically. The biggest polluters are Japan and Australia and the industrialized nations in North America and Europe. For instance, the United States alone was responsible for around 23 percent of global CO_2 emissions in 1998.

Poorer nations in the developing world currently produce smaller volumes of the major pollutants. At present, these nations are often more concerned about the problems of indoor smoke pollution from the burning of biomass fuels (such as wood, charcoal, and animal dung). However, as their industries develop and people become wealthy enough to buy motor vehicles and other consumer goods, they will generate greater air pollution.

The fact that the richest 20 percent of the world produces 63 percent of CO_2 emissions, compared to just 2 percent produced by the poorest 20 percent, suggests that some countries are responsible for much more air pollution than others. However, this pattern is changing. As wealthy nations introduce pollution controls and invest in cleaner technology, the developing world's contribution to air pollution will increase. For example, in 1990, developing countries contributed 30 percent to global CO_2 emissions but this increased to around 41 percent in 1998, and China is now the second biggest polluter after the United States.

A Chinese petrochemical plant: China's rapid industrial growth means that it may soon become the world's biggest contributor of CO_2 emissions.

Dirty Cities

More and more people around the world are living in towns and cities and their activities generate many pollutants in a relatively small area. This means that the air in our towns and cities is often full of pollutants that can damage our health and buildings. Urban air pollution is particularly bad in the developing world, in cities such as Cairo, Egypt; Mexico City, Mexico; and Jakarta, Indonesia. This is partly because they use older technology that is often dirtier than modern equivalents, but can also be due to climatic conditions. Higher levels of sunlight encourage more photochemical reactions among the different pollutants, and weather patterns trap this polluted air close to the ground.

Children are especially vulnerable to air pollutants. These schoolgirls in Mexico City do what they can to protect their developing lungs.

Cities in developed countries are usually much cleaner, though they can still experience serious air pollution episodes. For example, in September 1997, Paris suffered such high levels of urban air pollution that the city authorities reduced the number of cars entering the city.

In developed countries, cities used to be much more polluted than they are today. Until the 1960s, many city-dwellers experienced high levels of SO_2 pollution due to their dependence on coal for heating their homes and producing electricity. SO_2 was one of the main pollutants in London, England's great smogs of 1952 and 1968 which killed around 4,700 people.

Clean Air Acts were passed in 1956 and 1968 to control the burning of coal in London and other cities, and many homes have since been converted to gas central heating which does not emit SO_2. As a result, SO_2 emissions from cities in Great Britain have fallen by more than 60 percent since 1960. Most developed nations have similar policies that have made cities more pleasant and much healthier to live in.

Trafalgar Square, in London, England, on an October mid-afternoon. Pollution from coal used in heating caused several such pollution episodes until the mid-1960s.

The problem for cities in developing countries is that they are growing very rapidly, which makes it difficult for the authorities to control their emissions. Such rapid development needs large amounts of energy and this often comes from polluting fossil fuels. In China for example, around 75 percent of energy is produced using "brown coal" which emits high levels of SO_2 when it is burned. It is possible to prevent the SO_2 from entering the atmosphere, but this increases the cost of electricity production by at least 15 percent and many poorer nations cannot afford this.

Monitoring Urban Air Pollution

Since 1974 the World Health Organization (WHO) and the United Nations Environment Program (UNEP) have monitored urban air pollution in fifty cities across thirty-five countries. Seven main pollutants—including SO_2, CO_2, NO_2, and particulate matter—are measured and the WHO has set health guidelines for each of these so that we can protect our health.

Monitoring can help prevent illness or death such as that caused by the New York and London smogs during the 1960s. In the last thirty years, levels of air pollution have fallen to safer levels in most developed nations, but cities in developing countries such as Beijing, China and Sao Paulo, Brazil have levels above WHO guidelines and in many cities they are getting worse. In Mexico City, it is estimated that air pollution is 100 times above safe levels. China is the worst country overall; it has seven of the ten most polluted cities in the world.

Santiago, Chile has been fighting a losing battle against pollution from vehicles and industry. A thick blanket of smog is an almost daily feature of the skyline.

Particulate Matter

The worst air pollutant affecting cities today is particulate matter which often exceeds WHO guidelines by more than 200 percent. Asian cities—in countries such as China, Indonesia, and the Philippines—are especially affected because of their rapid increase in vehicle numbers and their limited control of industrial emissions.

Asthma affects an increasing number of children and young people and there are fears that it may be linked to greater levels of air pollution.

High levels of particulate matter are known to harm people's health and in extreme cases even cause death. The tiny particles released by vehicle exhausts, industrial chimneys, and domestic energy use enter people's lungs when they breathe. They can damage the lungs, making breathing difficult and leading to illnesses such as asthma, bronchitis, and heart disease. Exposure over a long period can eventually lead to certain types of cancer.

In the United Kingdom particulate matter is thought to cause 10,000 deaths per year and in the United States it is known to aggravate asthma which affects an estimated 4.8 million children there. In fact, asthma is the main illness causing children to be absent from school in the United States. In developing countries, the problems associated with particulate matter are made worse because they often lack the health facilities to treat people suffering from such illnesses.

National Action

Emissions from vehicle exhausts pose a particular risk to children, although lead-free gasoline has reduced this in recent years.

Governments have come up with various ways to reduce air pollution and most countries now have special departments to monitor levels and enforce laws. One such department is the Environmental Protection Agency (EPA) in the United States which was created in 1970 to monitor and enforce the Clean Air Act. The EPA has since added new laws and guidelines to further improve air quality and has been very successful in tackling certain pollutants. EPA policies to remove lead from gasoline, for example, have reduced lead air pollution by 98 percent and cut lead levels in children's blood by 75 percent since 1970.

Many countries enforce the use of newer technology such as scrubbers, which are fitted to power plants to remove pollutants before they enter the atmosphere. Catalytic converters are another example. Combined with improved fuels (unleaded gasoline, liquid petroleum gas or LPG, and city diesel), vehicles built today produce 95 percent less pollution than those made in 1970. However, the number of vehicles on the world's roads has increased by more than 260 percent over the same period, so vehicle pollution is still a major problem.

Taxation is another way that governments can try to control air pollution, by making producers of pollution pay higher taxes than those using cleaner technologies. In Norway, for example, the government introduced a tax on older cars and paid for less efficient and more polluting vehicles to be junked. This resulted in 211,000 vehicles being junked in 1996 (compared to around 60,000

VIEWPOINTS

"Impose the cost of pollution on people who breathe, so the people who pollute can avoid the cost of control. I think that is backwards."
Edmund S. Muskie, former U.S. Senator

"People are clearly upset by the surging prices [of gasoline]. But there's no indication that the sentiment is in fact causing people to drive less."
Geoff Sundstrom, American Automobile News

Sustainable transportation such as bicycles and trams (seen here in Amsterdam, Holland) can help reduce air pollution.

before the tax was introduced). In the United Kingdom new cars bought since March 2001 have been taxed according to the pollution they produce. Taxes like these help to make consumers and manufacturers more aware of their role in managing air pollution.

Some governments take a more direct approach in informing the public about air pollution. For instance, city authorities in Europe can choose to hold a car-free day each September to encourage people to use public transportation or walk or bicycle instead of driving. In 1999, sixty-six French towns took part in a "car-free day" and local levels of major pollutants fell by as much as 50 percent as a result.

SO₂ Emissions in Europe and North America 1980–2010 (Thousands of tons)

Country	1980	1985	1990	1995	2000*	2005*	2010*
Canada	4643	3692	3236	2681	2833	2914	2914
Czech Republic	2257	2277	1876	1091	462	421	376
Denmark	450	339	182	150	90	90	-
France	3338	1470	1250	958	868	770	737
Germany	7514	7732	5313	2102	1300	990	550
Italy	3757	1901	1651	1322	1004	847	842
United Kingdom	4863	3729	3731	2351	1290	1020	850
United States	23501	21074	20989	16830	15614	16250	16235
Yugoslavia	406	478	508	462	680	889	1135

NB: Germany 1980 and 1985 East and West figures combined

* predicted emissions   Source: EMEP

FACT

Urban areas, where polluting industries and traffic are most severe, are also often areas of high population. In Europe, 80 percent of the population lives in urban areas.

DEBATE

Do you think it is important to control the amounts of air pollution produced in countries, cities, and towns? Why do you think some countries are not doing that much to protect their environment?

LOCAL AIR POLLUTION

Smoke from a barbecue may make the food taste good but it also adds to local pollution. Using one barbecue for many people as shown here, near Mount St. Helens, can help reduce this pollution.

Air Pollution Starts at Home

Even though so much attention is focused on international issues, such as global warming and acid rain, the pollutants that cause these global problems are usually a result of our own activities in our homes, schools, and offices. Each time we switch on a light we use electricity which has probably caused pollution while it has been generated. Every car trip produces emissions, and even our trash causes air pollution as it is burned in an incinerator or decomposes in a landfill site and emits methane gas. It is vital for all of us to understand what causes local air pollution in order to help reduce it.

Local Air Pollutants

Air pollution can be very local, such as the smoke from a cigarette or a barbecue in someone's back-yard. Noises, such as those made by a barking dog or a neighbor's loud music, are also types of local air pollution. Smell, like noise, is often ignored as a type of air pollutant, despite the fact that certain smells can be extremely unpleasant, making us feel sick or breathless.

Many pollutants are produced inside the buildings where we live and work and this is known as indoor air pollution. Fumes from stoves and heaters, dust and traffic exhaust blown in through open windows, chemicals from cosmetics and cleaning products, and even dead skin cells from people, are all types of indoor air pollution. But some are of greater concern than others. For example, some cleaning products may contain volatile organic compounds (VOCs). These evaporate into the air, contribute to illnesses such as asthma and increase the risk of cancer. Scientists have found that VOC levels can be ten times higher inside buildings than they are in the open air.

A recent cause for concern has been the growing use of incinerators for waste disposal. As the waste is burned, it produces toxic pollutants such as dioxins, which are known to be linked to around 7 percent of cancers. Modern incinerators are cleaner than the old ones, but many local residents are still worried about the effect that air pollution may have on their health. In the United Kingdom, for example, experts have suggested that up to 350 deaths per year may be caused if plans go ahead to build seventy new incinerators by 2025.

VIEWPOINTS

"Incinerators reduce the volume of waste by about 90 percent, a significant reduction of waste that would otherwise go into a landfill."
Environmental Literacy Council

"You don't get rid of the trash, you just change its nature and disperse a lot of it to the wind. It's a dangerous process."
Vyvyan Howard, a toxicopathologist at Liverpool University, in England

The manure being used on this German farm produces air pollutants that can be smelled by those living nearby.

FACT

Radon is the second highest cause of lung cancer deaths in the United States after smoking.

Some natural pollutants can leak into buildings through cracks and remain trapped in the still air inside. Radon is one of these and is of particular concern because it is radioactive. It can cause cancer if people are exposed to it for long periods.

Methane gas is another natural pollutant created as organic materials decompose. Methane can leak into buildings constructed on landfill sites as the trash rots under the ground. Special vents are normally constructed to release the methane into the atmosphere and avoid a dangerous build-up. But this does not solve the global problem because methane is also a major greenhouse gas.

Effects of Indoor Pollutants

We know that outdoor air pollution can be bad for our health but it is estimated that people in regions such as the United States and northern Europe spend 90 percent of their time indoors. Scientists who study indoor air pollution have found that levels of some pollutants are often two to five times higher than they are outside. And in extreme cases they could be as much as 100 times greater. Exposure to indoor air pollutants is thought to have increased in many developed countries due to modern building methods. Double glazed windows help to keep buildings warm and save energy. But, as well as trapping heat, they also trap pollutants.

One indoor pollutant that particularly affects children's health is tobacco smoke. Second-hand smoke contains around 4,000 chemicals, including carbon monoxide,

One of the most common and harmful indoor pollutants is cigarette smoke. Breathing it in ("passive smoking") can even lead to cancer.

nicotine, and tar. Many of these are hazardous to human health, affecting our breathing, irritating our eyes, and causing cancer. Children breathing tobacco smoke are more likely to suffer from bronchitis and other chest infections and are at greater risk of developing asthma. In the United States alone, tobacco smoke is thought to worsen the condition of up to 1 million asthmatic children.

VOCs from cleaning products, paints, or solvents can also affect our health, making our eyes, nose, and lungs hurt and sometimes making us feel dizzy or sick. Many products containing VOCs now carry warnings to open windows and ensure that there is plenty of fresh air before using them.

VIEWPOINT

"As the problems of outdoor air pollution have lessened in developed countries, more attention is now being given to the problems of indoor air environments."
G.B. Leslie and F.W. Lunan,
Indoor Air Pollution:
Problems and Priorities, 1992

People working indoors with sprays need to protect themselves from pollutants.

Indoor Pollutants in Developing Countries

In developing countries the main form of indoor air pollution is smoke from the use of biomass fuels in cooking. Wood, crop waste, charcoal, and even dried animal dung are used as fuel on basic open stoves, similar to a barbecue.

Smoke pollution from wood stoves irritates the eyes and can make breathing difficult. But for this Tu woman in Qinghai, China, there is little choice.

Used outside, the combination of many stoves can create neighborhood pollution problems. But the greatest effects are felt when cooking is done inside, especially during the rains or in the cooler evenings. Most stoves lack chimneys or vents to remove pollutants and so they build up quickly inside the home. Women are especially affected by this because they do most of the cooking but so are young children, who spend much of their time with their mothers. Estimates suggest that two million people die each year due to illnesses caused by this form of air pollution. India alone recorded around 500,000 deaths per year during the 1990s. Many more suffer from poor eyesight, blindness, and breathing difficulties that make it hard for them to work or study properly.

Reducing Indoor Air Pollution

Because indoor air pollution is local, there are many things we can do to reduce it. We can make sure people smoke outside, or better yet try to help them give up smoking altogether. We can check the products we buy to make sure they do not have high levels of VOCs. (Many products now contain this information on their packaging to help us make these choices.) Kitchens can be fitted with extractor fans to remove air pollutants without having to let cold air—or outside pollutants—in.

Even when we have to use products that we know create indoor pollutants we can do a great deal to protect our health. For instance, it's obviously best to open the window when you are using paints or glues and wear a protective face mask if doing a dusty job such as sanding. We can also think about when we do certain jobs. For example, stripping and waxing a school floor would be best planned for a Friday after school, so that by Monday morning, when the children return, any pollutants will have dispersed.

In developing countries, indoor pollution can be reduced by using improved fuels such as kerosene or liquid petroleum gas (LPG) that produce less smoke than biomass fuels. Educating people to keep children away from the cooking area would reduce their exposure to the harmful effects of smoke. Building a chimney to help carry the smoke away could also reduce pollutant levels and improve health.

VIEWPOINT

"...global ill-health from air pollution may well be dominated by the effects of indoor exposure in developing countries."
Kirk Smith, School of Public Health, University of California

In villages like this one in rural Ghana, West Africa, local air pollution can reach high levels when everyone cooks their meals.

However, the smoke from open fires helps to preserve the grasses used in thatched roofs and keeps mosquitoes away. If this smoke was removed or reduced, it could lead to an increase in diseases such as malaria which is carried by mosquitoes.

Think Globally, Act Locally

At the 1992 Earth Summit, governments agreed to plans that would encourage people in their own neighborhoods to become involved in local projects that would help protect the global environment. This plan is called Agenda 21 and its main message is to "Think Globally, Act Locally."

There are things we could all do at a local level that would help counteract international problems such as global warming or acid rain. Some of these things are very simple, such as turning lights off when they are not needed and using energy-efficient light bulbs. Others may need more planning and investment, such as improving the insulation of buildings so that they use less energy for heating.

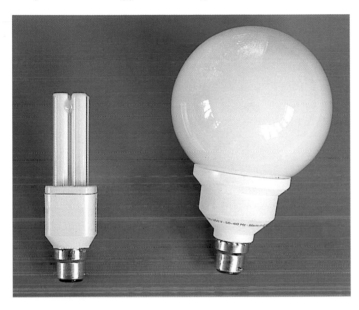

Energy-efficient light bulbs can reduce household contributions to air pollution significantly.

Attitudes are also important. For instance, you could decide to walk or ride a bicycle to go short distances instead of using a vehicle. If you must use a vehicle then use public transportation such as buses. A single bus carries about the same number of people as ten full cars, but takes up about a quarter of the road space.

Encouraging others to think about their local contributions to air pollution could also help. For instance, you might be able to work with your school to reduce air pollution and save energy. Even simple actions, such as sharing car trips with friends, or better yet walking, will make a difference. Don't forget that these actions can also save money and improve your health.

FACT

In heavy traffic jams, the air quality can be poorer inside the car than out. Car users regularly suffer up to three times as much pollution as pedestrians.

DEBATE

Do you think it's important to reduce indoor air pollution? How would you reduce the amounts of indoor air pollution you produce?

TECHNOLOGY AND CLEANER AIR

Cleaning The Air

FACT

City diesel is a low emission type of diesel that was developed in Sweden. In comparison to normal diesel, it produces less sulphur dioxide and particulate matter.

We have learned about the many different types of air pollution we face and have looked at predictions that tell us things are getting worse. However, we have also seen how improved technologies have allowed us to reduce certain types of pollution considerably. New national and international targets have been set to make sure that air pollution is reduced. And higher taxes for polluters have encouraged manufacturers and consumers to think and act cleaner.

This is all very encouraging, but many environmentalists say that we are not doing enough. They argue that major changes are needed in the way we live if we are to seriously reduce air pollution from today's levels. They also argue that we cannot afford to wait any longer because, even if major changes were made today, the long-term effects of air pollution would still be felt for many years.

Many governments are building bicycle tracks to encourage greater use of bicycles, as in this street scene in Denmark. Similar lanes for buses often give them priority over cars.

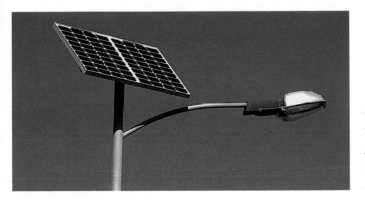

Solar power can be especially useful in more remote areas. This panel provides power for a streetlight in Lanzarote, one of the Canary Islands off the West African coast.

Short- and Long-term Measures

These different approaches can be roughly split into short-term and long-term measures. Short-term measures are those that reduce levels of pollutants immediately, such as removing lead from gasoline or fitting filters to power plants' chimneys. Long-term measures aim to remove the pollutants altogether. They include the greater use of renewable energy, such as the sun to power solar cars, or the wind to generate electricity, or changing our lifestyle to reduce our energy consumption. It is not always easy to make these changes, though, and many governments are concerned that making them too suddenly could cause economic problems.

Environmentalists, however, argue that the cost of adopting long-term measures is often far lower than the expense of dealing with the diseases and environmental damage caused by our current level of air pollution.

Energy Demand

We all use energy in our everyday lives and in most countries this energy is generated using fossil fuels such as coal, oil, and gas. We depend on these resources, even though we know they pollute our atmosphere. And our dependence has increased dramatically, with world fossil fuel usage growing by over 470 percent between 1950 and 1998.

FACT

In the United States, the number of people using private vehicles to get to work increased from 41.4 million in 1960 to 99.6 in 1990.

VIEWPOINTS

"Emission cuts agreed at Kyoto will not be feasible without a clear application of energy-saving techniques and renewable energies in the city environment."
Alberto Mitja, Head of the Catalan Energy Institute, Spain

"I believe we already have the technology but the question is how we deploy it in the city of tomorrow."
Gustaf Landahl, Stockholm city official and co-ordinator of Zero and Low Emission Vehicles in an Urban Society (ZEUS)

FACT

In the U.S., wind power already provides enough electricity for 1 million Americans.

VIEWPOINTS

"One of the limitations of wind power is that it is only available when the wind blows, so you can't have anything powered by wind at 100 percent."
Randall Swisher, American Wind Energy Association

"Wind Powering America will double U.S. wind capacity by 2005, and double it again by 2010 to create enough energy to fulfill the annual energy needs of three million households."
Bill Richardson, former U.S. Secretary of Energy

Urban pollution episodes in the 1960s and the discovery of acid rain damage in the 1970s forced governments to look at ways to make energy production cleaner. Scrubbers were an early technological answer and were fitted to many coal-fired power plants to remove sulphur dioxide and nitrogen dioxide emissions before they entered the atmosphere. Modern scrubbers remove up to 95 percent of emissions, but increase the cost of a new power station by up to 20 percent. There is also the problem of how to dispose of the contaminated fluids used to remove the pollutants. An alternative answer adopted by several countries has been to convert power plants to use natural gas instead of coal to generate electricity. Although this is still a fossil fuel, it is less polluting than coal and does not emit sulphur, which is one of the main causes of acid rain.

In the longer term, environmentalists insist that energy will have to come from renewable sources such as the sun, wind, or water. This is not only because of concerns about air pollution, but also because fossil fuels are nonrenewable which means that they will eventually run out. Some experts predict that this could happen within the next 150 years.

Many forms of renewable energy are available today. Although their use is still small on a global scale, some countries have made great progress. Denmark, for example, leads the world in wind power technology, with a little over 8 percent of its electricity coming from wind farms in 1998. Danish firms are also responsible for more than half the world's exports of wind turbines and have formed partnerships with companies in countries such as Spain and India.

Solar power use is also growing as the photovoltaic (PV) cells that convert the sun's energy into electricity become cheaper to make. Solar power has been the cheapest form of power for remote areas for many years. For this reason, it has been used in many developing countries to power wells or provide electric light for isolated villages. Technological improvements mean that it is now possible to build roofs made of PV cells and use them to generate the energy needs of the building. Schemes to install a million such roofs by the year 2010 have been launched in the United States and parts of Europe.

Spain is among the world leaders in wind power—likely to be a major form of renewable energy in the future.

Growth in Wind Power 1980–1998

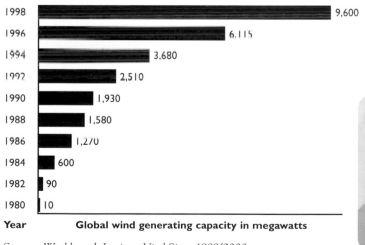

Year	Global wind generating capacity in megawatts
1998	9,600
1996	6,115
1994	3,680
1992	2,510
1990	1,930
1988	1,580
1986	1,270
1984	600
1982	90
1980	10

Source: *Worldwatch Institute Vital Signs 1999/2000*

VIEWPOINT

"Natural gas is a scarce resource and will be depleted within 60 years at present consumption rates."
Rosa Filippini, Friends of the Earth, Italy

The Nuclear Question

In addition to renewable energy sources, several countries have invested in nuclear power to meet their energy demands. Nuclear energy costs less than fossil fuel energy and produces none of the normal pollutants. Thus, it was welcomed as a technological breakthrough in the 1950s, and by 1998 some 429 nuclear power plants were operating in countries such as Germany, France, Japan, the United States, the United Kingdom, India, and China. The problem with nuclear energy is that it produces large quantities of hazardous radioactive waste which must be carefully treated and stored for up to 100,000 years.

Nuclear power normally produces few air pollutants, but one accident could have devastating effects.

Environmentalists had long criticized governments for investing in nuclear power, claiming that it was unsafe and could lead to an environmental and human disaster. Then, in 1986, an accident at the Chernobyl nuclear reactor in the former Soviet Union appeared to confirm their fears. A cloud of radioactive material was blown into the air and carried across most of western and northern Europe. Meat, milk, and vegetables were contaminated, and much produce had to be thrown away. In the area around the reactor, over 3,107 square miles (5,000 square kilometers) of land had to be evacuated and an estimated 10,000 people have since died due to the effects of radiation.

After Chernobyl many governments stopped building nuclear reactors, and Austria, Sweden, and Italy decided to close their existing reactors. In some

VIEWPOINT

"I can envisage somewhere about 2050, when the greenhouse really begins to bite...people will start looking back and saying: 'whose fault was all this?' And they will settle on the environmentalists and say: 'if those damn people hadn't stopped us [from] building nuclear power stations we wouldn't be in this mess.' And I think it is true."
James Lovelock, environmental theorist

developing countries, however, nuclear energy is still in favor. New reactors are being built in India and there are plans in China to build fifty by the year 2020.

Governments have to decide if the risk of accidents like Chernobyl is worth taking, compared to the damage caused by the continued use of fossil fuels. It has been proved that nuclear energy can be very clean, but a single accident could produce such catastrophic air pollution that many people now believe it is not worth taking the risk.

FACT

Following the Chernobyl accident in 1986, farm animals in Denmark and Sweden were kept indoors for a whole year to avoid contamination.

Radioactive fallout from Chernobyl was carried quickly across Europe by climatic air currents.

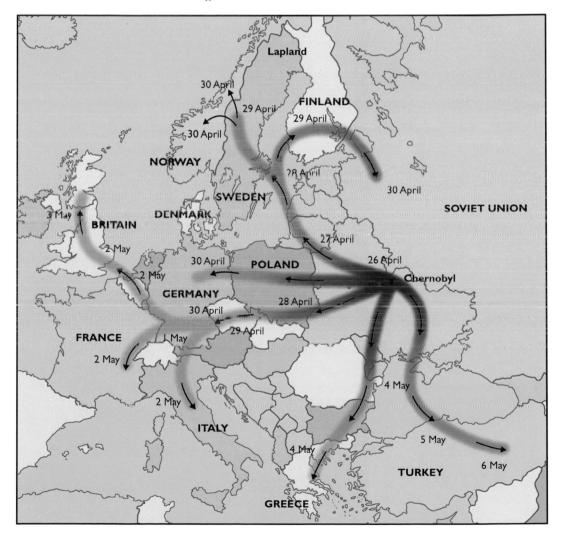

Vehicle Pollution

Motor vehicles are said to be responsible for 16 percent of acid rain and 10 percent of greenhouse gas emissions. Unfortunately, with over 100,000 new

cars being manufactured every day, air pollution from vehicles is likely to become even worse. Although technology has reduced pollution from individual vehicles considerably over the past thirty years, the benefit is often outweighed by the overall increase in the number of vehicles. Developing countries face particular problems, as vehicles are often older or poorly maintained. Even their newer vehicles cause pollution because they use less purified fuels and the laws controlling emissions are normally less strict.

Despite cleaner technology, growth in car sales means overall vehicle pollution is increasing in some parts of the world. In Korea, car ownership has recently boomed.

As we have seen, the introduction of unleaded gasoline reduced lead pollution by 98 percent in the United States alone, and this shows that relatively small changes can sometimes have a dramatic effect. Most European countries now use unleaded gasoline as standard, but in many parts of the developing world unleaded gasoline is not yet available.

Catalytic Converters

Catalytic converters have also reduced vehicular air pollution. These were first introduced in the 1970s in the United States and Japan and since 1993 they have been fitted to all new cars in the European Union. A catalytic converter, or CAT, is a special box fitted to the exhaust system of a vehicle. Waste gases leave the engine and pass through the CAT where platinum metals cause chemical reactions to convert them into less harmful emissions.

Catalytic converters can reduce emissions of carbon monoxide, hydrocarbons, and nitrogen oxides by as much as 80 percent, but only if they reach a temperature between 300 and 400°C. On short trips, converters do not always reach this temperature and so levels of air pollution remain similar to a vehicle without a converter.

This problem is caused by people's behavior rather than the technology—the solution would be to walk or ride a bike to go such short distances. However, even when they work properly, catalytic converters are still a short-term measure. Carbon monoxide, for example, is turned into carbon dioxide by the converter and therefore adds to the problem of global warming.

FACT

The number of privately owned motor vehicles in Korea increased by an incredible 2,216 percent between 1980 and 1996!

Exhaust gases from the engine flow through a catalytic converter. They are converted by chemical reactions into less harmful emissions.

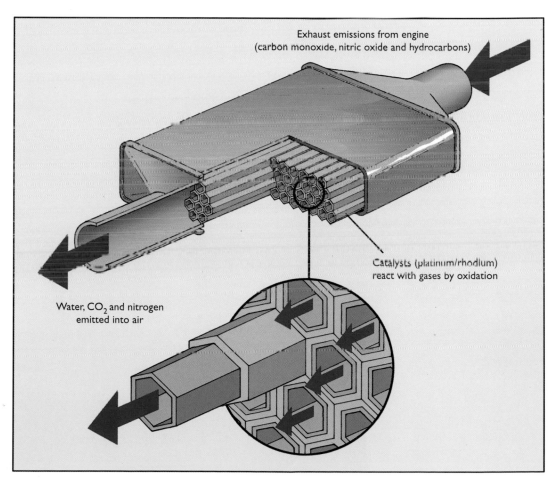

Exhaust emissions from engine
(carbon monoxide, nitric oxide and hydrocarbons)

Catalysts (platinum/rhodium)
react with gases by oxidation

Water, CO_2 and nitrogen
emitted into air

Hydrogen-powered vehicles like this bus in Vancouver, Canada, are seen by many as the most likely replacement for the combustion engine in today's vehicles.

Sustainable Transportation

Catalytic converters, unleaded fuel, city diesel, and more efficient engines have all helped to reduce air pollution from vehicles, but they are not long-term measures. In the long term, alternative fuels must be found. Some vehicles already use alternative fuels such as electricity or solar power. The problem is that they are often expensive, slow, and unable to travel over great distances without being recharged.

Hybrid vehicles, such as the Toyota Prius, offer one solution to this. The engine is part gasoline and part electric, and a computer system switches between the two power sources according to the speed of the vehicle. In slow traffic the electric

engine is used which is quiet and produces no air pollution. As the car speeds up, the gasoline engine takes over since it is more efficient at higher speeds. The really clever thing about hybrid engines is that when the gasoline engine is working, it recharges the batteries for the electric motor so that there is no need to plug it in for recharging as with earlier electric vehicles.

Forecasting Technology

In recent years, technology has dramatically improved our ability to measure and monitor levels of air pollution and their sources. Using sophisticated computer programs, this technology can even be used to predict air pollution episodes. Just as meteorologists can predict what the weather will be like for the next few days, scientists studying air pollution can warn us if pollutants are reaching dangerous levels.

This information is particularly useful to people who suffer from breathing difficulties and illnesses such as asthma and bronchitis. They are able to check their local air quality and take extra medicines, or if it is very bad they may even choose to stay indoors. Governments can also take action, as done in Greece and France, where the number of vehicles allowed into major cities is reduced when high air pollution levels are expected.

Technology Is Not the Solution

Although technology can help us to live with and reduce air pollution, it only makes a difference if people use it. Many people resist change and this has led environmentalists to say that technology alone is not the solution. We must also change—or be made to change—our behavior, if we seriously want to improve the situation.

VIEWPOINTS

"The rapid advancement of renewable, clean, energy sources must be THE priority for governments if we are to avert ecological catastrophe."
Dr. Jeremy Leggett, Chief Executive, Solar Century (British solar energy company)

"Simple technical fix solutions may fail to absorb the impacts of a growing population, de-vegetated land use changes, and economic growth in developing economies that are creating new sources of greenhouse gases."
Tim O'Riordan and Andrew Jordan, Center for Social and Economic Research on the Global Environment, University of East Anglia, United Kingdom

DEBATE

Do you think technology will remove the problem of air pollution or will it just reduce the amounts we produce? Can we depend on technology alone to tackle problems such as global warming?

RESPONSIBILITY FOR AIR POLLUTION

Who Will Lead the Way?

Cleaner technologies are often more expensive than polluting ones, and people are not always prepared to pay for them even when they understand the benefits. Electricity produced by solar cells, for example, costs up to five times more than when it is carried by towers in a grid network. Similarly, energy-saving products such as economical washing machines or fuel-efficient cars can cost significantly more than their less efficient alternatives. Unfortunately, in a free market, many consumers choose the cheaper option to save money.

Our homes could be more environmentally friendly. This eco-home in Denmark recycles water, saves energy, and uses solar and wind energy to generate power.

The problem is how to encourage people to use technologies that will reduce air pollution. Governments often support consumer choice and suggest that if people demand cleaner products then manufacturers will provide them. But many environmentalists argue that this is too simple. They suggest imposing a system of taxes and incentives to make cleaner products cheaper and those that produce high levels of air pollution more expensive. In reality, we probably need to combine both approaches. The question is who will lead the way—government, manufacturers, or consumers?

The Polluter Pays Principle

In recent years, governments have introduced a wide range of taxes to help control air pollution and meet international emission targets. A good example is the introduction of a tax on leaded gasoline in the United Kingdom. In 1988, just 1 percent of private cars used unleaded fuel. Once taxes made leaded fuel comparatively more expensive than unleaded, unleaded fuel use increased to 25 percent by the end of 1989.

FACT

The Swedish tax on NOx was the main cause of a 35 percent emissions reduction in a single year.

Even renewable sources of electricity such as the Itaipu hydroelectric dam in Brazil can produce air pollution, since rotting vegetation in the reservoir produces methane.

The idea is that the more air pollution you generate, the more you pay. This is known as the "Polluter Pays Principle" and it is now commonly used as a basis for controlling air pollution. In Denmark, for example, a sulphur tax was introduced in 1996. This tax varies according to the level of sulphur emitted. It costs polluters $1.13 for each kilogram of SO_2 emitted. This means that industries using high-sulphur fuels, such as coal, will have to pay more to produce their goods than those using sulphur-free energy such as wind power or natural gas.

VIEWPOINT

"It is possible to get very angry and dismayed about what we are doing to the world but it does not help. What matters is being constructive and realizing that where there is political will, much can be achieved."
Dr. Topfer, former German Environment Minister

There is a limit to how much people will pay, however. In September 2000, consumers in England and Wales brought roads to a standstill to protest about the high price of gasoline and diesel. This action surprised many people and was considered a warning to governments and environmentalists who might try to tax fuels such as gasoline in order to help pay for a cleaner environment.

Incentives

Another way to reduce air pollution is to give incentives to individuals and companies to use cleaner methods. Incentives often take the form of subsidies, which are a bit like taxes except that they give you money rather than take it away. In Japan, a government subsidy on PV cells led to a boom in sales of solar technology, with

British truck drivers protested against the cost of fuel in September 2000.

more than 6,800 rooftop systems being installed in 1998 alone. The United States is considering a similar subsidy to reduce the cost of new solar roof systems by 15 percent as an incentive to consumers and businesses.

A subsidy on wind power in the United States saw wind generation increase by 226 megawatts in 1998 (accounting for more than 10 percent of the global increase that year). Germany and Spain have also introduced wind power incentives and in Spain's northern industrial region of Navarra, wind energy now provides 20 percent of local electricity.

Warmcel insulation (recycled newspaper) sprayed into the walls of new homes can considerably reduce energy use, and therefore pollution.

VIEWPOINT

"Taxes on motorists should be tripled to reflect the true cost of road transportation, which adds 11 billion pounds a year to health bills because of exhaust pollution."
The British Lung Foundation

Incentives can also be offered to home owners. In the United Kingdom, for example, the government offers financial support to help people insulate their homes properly. A well-insulated home could reduce heating costs by up to 50 percent, and because energy is used more efficiently, air pollution is also reduced.

Incentives Cost Money

One of the problems with incentives is that someone has to pay for them. In developed countries, polluting technology is often taxed to subsidize cleaner methods, but for many developing countries it's not so simple. Developing countries are usually trying to encourage new businesses; the introduction of taxes or tight pollution controls might cause people to invest elsewhere. They can rarely afford to offer subsidies either, so in many cases they have little choice but to allow companies to use the technology they choose, even if it is more polluting.

VIEWPOINT

"Governments should be leading the way to a fundamentally new energy direction based on clean renewable energy like wind or solar power. But at present, many governments instead use taxpayers' money to support the agenda of companies which continue to spend billions of dollars on development of coal, oil, gas—the climate-damaging fossil fuels."
Greenpeace website

Industries based in the developed world have sometimes taken advantage of this and built factories in countries where pollution controls and taxes are less strict. In this way they can make the same products for less and then import them back into their own countries to sell. However, pollution generated during the production process is suffered by people living near the factories. The consumers who benefit from cheaper goods do not normally suffer and are probably unaware of the pollution and suffering they might be supporting.

Consumer Power

If consumers become aware of the pollution caused by the goods and services they purchase then they can help reduce air pollution by making different choices about what they buy and use. Consumer power can be highly effective in encouraging manufacturers to change to cleaner production methods.

In the 1990s, environmental groups were very active in making people aware of the pollution their lifestyles were causing. Their actions led to a rapid increase in demand for environmentally friendly products and gave rise to "green consumerism." So successful was this movement that consumers can now buy books that list "green" products and in some towns there are shops that only sell products made by green manufacturers.

Recycling materials such as paper conserves resources, but transporting them long distances can produce numerous pollutants and may make the benefits questionable.

Many manufacturers now advertise the fact that their goods are less polluting with special symbols such as the "Energy Star" on electrical goods made in the United States or the "Blue Angel" on German products. Systems like these help us choose products that are less polluting, and if more people buy them, other manufacturers are encouraged to join such schemes. Labelling systems are particularly effective when there is little extra cost in buying the less polluting option. For example, most Energy Star products cost little more than competing brands. And by choosing to buy these products an average American household could save $400 on their annual energy bills.

Consumers can also reduce energy use and air pollution by recycling their waste and buying goods made of recycled materials. Recycling aluminium drink cans, for example, uses up to 95 percent less energy and produces 95 percent fewer greenhouse gases than making aluminium with raw materials.

FACT

If everyone in the United States bought products labeled with the Energy Star for their homes and offices over the next fifteen years, then energy worth almost $100 billion would be saved.

Most of us can recycle materials—such as glass—close to our homes at special collection points. This small effort can have a big effect over time.

International Responsibilities

Many air pollutants cause problems far from their source and these demand special forms of responsibility that might involve several countries, or in the case of issues such as global warming, the entire world. To help countries meet their responsibilities to each other, various international organizations have been established to coordinate policies and decide on emissions targets.

One such organization is the United Nations Economic Commission for Europe (UNECE) which was set up in the late 1970s to tackle trans-boundary air pollution such as SO_2. Under the leadership of Norway and Sweden (the countries most affected by acid rain) the "30 percent club" was formed in 1984. This aimed to cut SO_2 emissions to 30 percent below 1980 levels by 1993.

By April 1985, 19 countries had agreed to these targets, although the United Kingdom (which was one of the worst polluters) initially refused to sign the agreement. The target of 30 percent was met by all the countries involved and in many cases they exceeded it. Austria, for example, managed to cut emissions by 82 percent and even the United Kingdom managed a 35 percent reduction.

The United Nations Framework Convention on Climate Change, signed at the Earth Summit in 1992 by over 160 countries, is the biggest agreement to control air pollution so far. At a second meeting in Kyoto, Japan in 1997, the same nations committed to reducing emissions of the six main greenhouse gases by 5.2 percent before 2012.

International cooperation does not always work, however, especially if one party is unwilling to enforce agreements. In Indonesia, for instance, farmers and companies have recently been clearing forests for agriculture and industry by burning them. Like other Southeast Asian countries, Indonesia has a zero burn policy that is supposed to ban such fires, but the government has failed to enforce this law. In 1997, Indonesian fires caused air pollution that affected the health of an estimated 70 million people in Indonesia, Malaysia, Singapore, the Philippines, Brunei, and Thailand. This demonstrates why countries should take their international responsibilities seriously. But it is often difficult for governments in developing countries such as Indonesia to control the actions of poor people who are just trying to earn a living.

Many Indonesians have been forced by poverty and a lack of opportunities to clear forests in order to grow crops. The resulting pollution can almost turn day into night.

DEBATE

Who should take responsibility for tackling the problem of air pollution? Should it be governments, industries, or ourselves, or do we all have roles to play? Who do you think should lead the way?

TOO LITTLE, TOO LATE?

The Challenge Ahead

As we have seen, air pollution affects us all—from local pollutants in our schools and homes to fears of climate change due to global warming and the erosion of the ozone layer. Technology and international efforts have helped reduce the problems caused by some pollutants (such as SO_2 and CFCs), but many still pose serious threats. Even now, new air pollutants are being created and scientists do not fully understand the effects they may have.

Jan Pronk, the Dutch Environment Minister, meets a protester at the United Nations Climate Conference at the Hague, November 2000. The sandbags symbolize the threat of floods due to global warming.

Because not all countries produce equal quantities of pollutants, deciding who is responsible and what should be done is very difficult. Environmentalists often complain that too much time is spent arguing over who should do what, and meanwhile the pollution is getting worse. The problem for governments is that committing themselves to reducing air pollution could increase production costs for their industries and make them less competitive in the global market. International agreements aim to overcome this problem, but many developing countries say it is unfair to expect them to meet the same targets as wealthier developed nations. India and China, for example, only agreed to cuts in CFC emissions when developed countries promised them financial help to develop alternatives.

Flooding, like this in Newport, Wales, in October 2000, is set to become a more common feature of life for many of us if climate change predictions come true.

Life on a Warmer Planet?

The biggest problem facing us today is the possibility of global warming. To prevent the predicted rise in global temperatures, scientists calculate that greenhouse gas emissions should be cut by 60 percent immediately. The 1997 Kyoto agreement to reduce emissions 5.2 percent by 2012 does not even come close to this figure.

So is global warming inevitable? According to leading experts we can now expect the atmosphere to warm by about 2.5°C by 2100 and by up to 6°C in countries such as Canada and Russia. But what will this mean for you or your children? You will probably experience more extreme weather patterns, such as heavy rains or long dry periods. You may be more at risk from diseases such as malaria or skin cancer due to greater exposure to the sun. If you live in Bangladesh, however, you could lose your home altogether. If sea levels rise as predicted, up to 6 million people in Bangladesh alone could be forced to move.

VIEWPOINTS

"You can't just say we had a flood in Mozambique and another in India and that must be down to global warming."
David Easterling, National Climate Data Center

"Probably the most dramatic and visible effect of global warming in the 21st or "greenhouse" century will be the rise in sea levels."
Nick Middleton, Geographical Magazine, United Kingdom

VIEWPOINTS

"...many challenges remain, and there are many different views on how best to ensure that we enjoy clean and healthy air, but considerable progress has been made."
Enviroliteracy website

"We're not reducing our greenhouse gas emissions anything like fast enough to stop the effects of climate change this century [...] We can slow warming down, but we can't stop it."
Chris Folland, Meteorological Office, UK, in New Scientist

VIEWPOINT

"...individuals can also help by changing some of their habits in quite simple ways. In combination, millions of individuals making such small changes can make a difference."
Nick Middleton, Geographical Magazine, United Kingdom

Is It Too Late?

If global warming is already happening then is it too late to do anything? Although many people may think so, it is important to consider what we can do. There are certain things that we cannot change, but if we were to stop trying altogether and carry on living as we do today then current carbon emissions of six billion tons could rise to as much as twenty billion in the next 100 years.

We need to solve the problems of air pollution so that people in developing regions can enjoy a better standard of living without further damaging the atmosphere. This idea is called sustainable development and this is the approach that environmentalists say we must adopt immediately. Progress can already be seen with increases in our use of renewable energy and higher rates of recycling, but there is still much to do.

Volunteers stacking materials for recycling into plastic bags.

What Can You Do?

You can do a great deal to help reduce air pollution in your own life. Turning off unnecessary lights, taking a shower instead of a bath, or walking to school instead of asking for a ride could all save energy and reduce emissions. You may not think these minor changes help much, but think about the combined effect of all your friends and neighbors doing the same.

Find out about any local organizations you could join, such as this city bicycle program in Denmark. You simply take a bicycle and then drop it off at your destination.

It's also important to help your friends and family to understand the causes of air pollution and how they could reduce it. For instance, you could encourage your parents to buy low or non-polluting products, or perhaps you could start a recycling program at school to reduce the energy used in collecting raw materials. Many communities already have environmental programs as part of the Agenda 21 agreements—you could find out how to get involved and maybe suggest new ideas.

You Have a Choice!

The most important thing to realize is that you have a choice when it comes to air pollution. This book has introduced you to some of the problems and solutions as well as the arguments about how best to move forward. There is much more you could learn. And the more information you have, the easier it will be to make choices. The main thing is not to leave those decisions to someone else—it's your future!

DEBATE

Think about all the changes that you and your family could make to reduce the amounts of air pollution you produce. Now think about how easy or difficult it would be to really make those changes. Do you think we will be able to tackle the problems of air pollution and make a cleaner future for ourselves?

GLOSSARY

acid rain this is formed when pollutants such as sulphur dioxide and nitrogen oxide mix with water vapor in the air to form an acidic solution. This solution falls to the ground as acid rain, damaging trees, lakes, and buildings.

atmosphere a mixture of gases surrounding the earth, made up of nitrogen (78.09 percent), oxygen (20.9 percent), argon (0.93 percent), hydrogen (0.05 percent) and carbon dioxide (0.03 percent), with small quantities of other gases, particles, and water vapor.

biomass fuels these are natural fuels that use plant or animal waste. They include wood, crop stalks, animal dung, and collected leaves. They are normally dried and burned, but animal dung can be used to produce a type of gas called biogas.

catalytic converter a filter fitted to a car exhaust to reduce harmful emissions such as carbon monoxide and nitric oxides. They are converted into less immediately harmful carbon dioxide, nitrogen, and water.

CFCs the abbreviation for a group of chemicals called Chlorofluorocarbons that destroy ozone in the atmosphere for up to one hundred years after they are released. They have been used in refrigerators, fire extinguishers and some aerosol sprays. Today their use is banned in new products.

developed countries the wealthier countries of the world, including Europe, North America, Japan, Australia, and New Zealand.

developing countries the poorer countries of the world, sometimes called the Third World, and including most of Africa, Asia, Latin America, and Oceania.

dioxins highly toxic chemical wastes produced during the manufacturing or disposal of products such as electrical goods and herbicides for controlling weeds. Dioxins can also be produced when incinerators do not fully burn plastic waste.

ecosystem the contents of an environment, including all the plants and animals that live there. This could be a garden pond, a forest, or the whole of planet earth.

emissions waste products (normally gases and solid particles) released into the atmosphere. These include car exhaust fumes and the wastes from chimneys at power plants and factories.

fossil fuels energy sources such as coal, oil, and gas formed millions of years ago by the fossilized remains of plants and animals.

global warming the gradual warming of the earth's atmosphere as a result of greenhouse gases trapping heat. Human activity has increased the level of greenhouse gases, such as carbon dioxide and methane, in the atmosphere.

greenhouse gas an atmospheric gas that traps some of the heat radiating from the earth's surface.

hydrocarbons a family of toxic air pollutants containing hydrogen and carbon that are released by fossil fuels and used in fuels, paints, solvents, and cleaning products. They include VOCs and PAHs (see separate Glossary entries).

methane a greenhouse gas produced by decomposing organic matter such as rotting vegetation or landfill sites. It is also a by-product of the digestive system of cows and of rice cultivation.

organic a product of living organisms that occurs naturally in the environment. Organic substances can be broken down by nature—they are biodegradable.

ozone there are two types of ozone, stratospheric and tropospheric ozone. Stratospheric ozone is found in the upper atmosphere and protects us from the sun's harmful ultraviolet rays. Tropospheric ozone is a pollutant made when sunlight, hydrocarbons, and nitrogen oxides react together in the lower atmosphere.

PAHs the abbreviation for a class of air pollutants called Polycyclic Aromatic Hydrocarbons which are emitted from vehicle exhausts.

particulate matter a type of air pollution that is made up of very small particles such as dust, soot, and smoke.

PCBs the abbreviation for a group of chemicals called Polychlorinatedbiphenyls used in electrical goods and some plastics. PCBs release dioxins if not properly disposed of in incinerators at over 1200°C.

PV cells the abbreviation for Photo Voltaic cells which convert the sun's energy into an electric current. They are used to provide power for electrical goods (calculators, watches, etc.), buildings and even the new international space station.

renewable energy sources energy sources that are easily replaced or replace themselves, to be used again (e.g., sun, wind, and water, used for solar, wind, and wave power). Fossil fuels are not renewable because they take millions of years to replace themselves.

scrubbers filters attached to chimney stacks to remove harmful gases by absorbing them in a liquid. In coal-fired power stations they are used to remove sulphur dioxide and reduce acid rain.

slurry a liquid containing a large quantity of solid material, normally like a thick paste. Farmyard slurry is diluted animal waste.

TOMPs the abbreviation for Toxic Organic Micro Pollutants. A group of pollutants produced by the incomplete burning of fuels or waste. They are highly toxic, even in small quantities, and some are carcinogenic. PCBs are one of the most important pollutants in this group.

VOCs the abbreviation for Volatile Organic Compounds. A group of pollutants emitted by vehicle exhausts and products such as paints and solvents.

BOOKS TO READ

Kidd, J.S., and Renee A. Kidd. *Into Thin Air: The Problem of Air Pollution*. New York: Facts on File, 1998.

Dolan, Edward F. *Our Poisoned Sky*. New York: Dutton Children's Books, 1991.

Bierhorst, John. *The Way of the Earth: Native America and the Environment*. New York: Morrow, William, & Co., 1994.

Preparing for a Career in the Environment. Chicago: Ferguson Publishing Co., 1998.

USEFUL ADDRESSES

http://www.epa.gov/students
The student pages of the United States
Environmental Protection Agency provide
information, facts, and data on environmental
issues including air pollution.

http://www.earthpreservers.com
This site is an environmental newspaper for
kids with contests, a virtual zoo, your
environmental questions answered by experts,
and other great links.

http://www.enviroliteracy.org
A very good educational site searchable by
topic and including air as a key category.
Provides its own information files with direct
links to information on other topical sites.

http://www.greenpeace.org
The website for the environmental action
group Greenpeace. Contains news and
information about current and past debates as
well as useful links to other organizations.

http://www.foe.org
The website for Friends of the Earth provides
information about current environmental
campaigns as well as links to other useful sites.

EPA Headquarters
Environmental Protection Agency
Ariel Rios Building
1200 Pennsylvania Avenue, NW
Washington, D.C. 20460
(202) 260-2090

Greenpeace USA
702 H Street NW, Suite 300
Washington, D.C. 20001
(202) 462-1177
email: greenpeace.usa@wdc.greenpeace.org

Friends of the Earth
1025 Vermont Avenue, NW
Washington, D.C. 20005
(877) 843-8687
email: foe@foe.org

INDEX

Numbers in **bold** refer to illustrations.